MOSAIC OF VOICES

Edited By Briony Kearney

First published in Great Britain in 2023 by:

Young Writers
Remus House
Coltsfoot Drive
Peterborough
PE2 9BF
Telephone: 01733 890066
Website: www.youngwriters.co.uk

All Rights Reserved
Book Design by Ashley Janson
© Copyright Contributors 2023
Softback ISBN 978-1-83565-027-1

Printed and bound in the UK by BookPrintingUK
Website: www.bookprintinguk.com
YB0572K

FOREWORD

For Young Writers' latest competition This Is Me, we asked primary school pupils to look inside themselves, to think about what makes them unique, and then write a poem about it! They rose to the challenge magnificently and the result is this fantastic collection of poems in a variety of poetic styles.

Here at Young Writers our aim is to encourage creativity in children and to inspire a love of the written word, so it's great to get such an amazing response, with some absolutely fantastic poems. It's important for children to focus on and celebrate themselves and this competition allowed them to write freely and honestly, celebrating what makes them great, expressing their hopes and fears, or simply writing about their favourite things. This Is Me gave them the power of words. The result is a collection of inspirational and moving poems that also showcase their creativity and writing ability.

I'd like to congratulate all the young poets in this anthology, I hope this inspires them to continue with their creative writing.

CONTENTS

Bervie School, Montrose

Kirsty Knight (10)	1
Sophie Richmond-Hawk (11)	2
Grace Adams (11)	4
Rihanna Ross (11)	6
Siena Burton (11)	8
Anna Marie Davies (11)	10
Euan Reid (10)	11
April Rowe (11)	12
Harvey Parley	13
Olivia Beedie	14
Micheal Crighton (11)	15
Amy Gray (11)	16
Logan Milne	17
Isla Craig (11)	18
Harrison Taylor (11)	19
Logan Bruce (10)	20
Poppy Lee Greig (11)	21
Luca Elders (11)	22
Linda-Frances Stubbs (10)	23
Lucy McElarney (11)	24
Abby Hogg (11)	25
Corrie Hillock (11)	26
Zoey Dziewientkowski-Rae	27
Georgia Paton (11)	28
Leo McNally (11)	29
Ethan Brooks (10)	30
Logan Meldrum	31
Jack Stephens (11)	32
Roxanne Taylor (11)	33
Isla Fergus (11)	34
Ellis Forshaw (10)	35
Jack Garrett (11)	36

Commercial Primary School, Dunfermline

Matilda Goring (9)	37
Sonny Husband (9)	38
Orla Healy (9)	40
Catalina Ionita (9)	42
Ollie Mitchell (9)	44
Malin Forrest (9)	45
Emily Pentleton (8)	46
Dylan Kinninmonth (9)	47
Aaron Leitch (9)	48
Dylan Devaney (9)	49
Lyra Fowles (9)	50
Imogen Fleetham (9)	51
Rory Mellon (9)	52
Lucas McLaughlin (9)	53
Ben Dumble (9)	54
Lyla Leader (9)	55
Hector Warner (9)	56
Toby Serkes (9)	57
Tehillah Isaiah (9)	58

Crail Primary School, Anstruther

Heather (10)	59
Ella Molly Drew (11)	60
Brodie Wilson (10)	62
Edward Robertson (10)	63
Euan Cochrane (10)	64
Julianna J (10)	65
Andy Grant (10)	66
Taylor B (10)	67
Matylda Kubecka (11)	68
Zach Taylor (11)	69
Kristians J (9)	70

Lewis Ireland (9)	71
Rupert (10)	72
Oscar F (9)	73
Lucas Yule (10)	74
Max M (10)	75

Gorsewood Primary School, Runcorn

Elli-Mae (9)	76
Millie Townsend (9)	77
Elle Woods (9)	78
Eliza Bennett (9)	79
Lenny Banks (9)	80
Erikka Pearson-Savage (9)	81
Tegan Probert Groom (10)	82
Hayley Neill (10)	83
Kylan Pearson-Savage	84
Charlie Sharp (9)	85
Jayden Yesilyurt (9)	86
Charlie Mitchell (9)	87
Laila Findlow (9)	88
Scarlett Disberry (9)	89
James Jones (9)	90
Karli Rotherham (9)	91
Logan Clarke (9)	92
Sophie Lawrence (8)	93

Harris Primary Academy Chafford Hundred, Grays

Rumaysa Suffyan (11)	94
Lucia Bushell (11)	96
Petar Borisov (10)	97
Kyla Ocean (10)	98
Carla Popa (9)	100
Kyron Mudhar (11)	101
Dovydas Dula (11)	102
Joannabel Emma Eshun (10)	103
Kouami Zewu-Manscour (10)	104
Karinna Maria Pirvu (10)	105
Mason McLintock (10)	106
Saanvi Bolisetty (10)	107
Zac Charova (10)	108

Jovani Junaid (9)	109
Idil Tunc (10)	110
Daisy Santos (10)	111
Nathan Chau (11)	112
Tanveer Khan (9)	113
Timilehion Rufai (11)	114
Casey Otieno (10)	115
Idris Akanbi (10)	116
George Raducanu (10)	117
Daniel Sosnowski (11)	118
James Michel Thomas (9)	119
Emily Georgieva (10)	120
Taqwa Khan (8)	121
Brielle Okparaocha (10)	122
Igor Karagiaz (11)	123
Oreida Pashaj (10)	124
Lewis Fern (10)	125
Adel Awoyemi (11)	126
Summer Dam (10)	127
Timas Miknevicius (10)	128
Leila Martynenko (11)	129
Sophie Chapman (11)	130
Helena Rose (10)	131
Michaela Somuyiva (11)	132
Poppy Maydell (10)	133
MJ Nee-Whang (10)	134
Dawud Shahzad (10)	135
Mahad Hassan (10)	136
Favor Mwafulirwa (10)	137
Ava Puri (10)	138
Harmony (10)	139
Ronnie Horning (11)	140
Ridwan Bada (10)	141
Frank Wojnarowski (10)	142
Arash Khan (10)	143
Abdul-Wadood Bello (10)	144
Hannas Aina (11)	145
Abhinav Chris Chakka (10)	146
Surayya Houssein (10)	147
Stefan Olaru (10)	148
Yasmin Al-Saadi (11)	149
Vakaris Niparavicius (11)	150
Kristupas Andriuska (10)	151

THE POEMS

This Is Me

I have a dog called Angus, he is my bundle of joy,
And Snowman is his favourite toy,
He is as fast as a lightning bolt, no matter what time of day,
Even when he is going fast, he always knows the way,
He is a cocker spaniel with ears as floppy as jelly,
Dad is always saying he has a big belly,
Granny's house is his favourite place and he's always a player,
Angus often runs upstairs when he's not meant to, so we call him the mischief-maker,
When he sleeps, he snores as loud as a lion's roar,
Getting louder and louder, causing a house war,
He loves to be down by the sea,
Where he is as mental as can be,
He can be a pest,
But no matter what he does, he will always be the best.

Kirsty Knight (10)
Bervie School, Montrose

This Is Me

I have light brown hair
My eyes are a deep blue
Baggy clothes are the things I love to wear
I have lots of freckles and some of them are new

Football is my favourite of all sports
I play defence and in goal
Baking cakes of all sorts
And I really love swinging on ropes

My favourite animal is an elephant
I love their long trunks and floppy ears
I really don't like foxes, even though they are very elegant
Foxes don't act the way they appear

Mum's peanut chicken is my favourite meal
It's so creamy and delicious
But Dad's cottage pie does not take my appeal
Even though Mum's risotto looks suspicious

My brother is annoying but sometimes sweet
My mum and dad are very kind

And sometimes they even give us treats
But they all love me which makes me super hyped

I have a dog called Dexter and he is a Labrador
He is very stupid and very goofy
And tries to fight with my 17-year-old cat in front of my bedroom door
My 17-year-old cat is called Oscar and when food is about he takes his opportunity.

Sophie Richmond-Hawk (11)
Bervie School, Montrose

This Is Me

Ingredients:
530g of height,
60g sportiness,
10g chatty,
80g of happiness,
70g of kindness,
A pinch of craziness,
A 100ml of red.

Instructions:
Step 1: In a large bowl, add the height and the kindness and stir well. In a separate bowl, beat the chatty and craziness until well combined.
Step 2: In the large bowl, add the sportiness, the happiness and the red and stir until well combined. Next whisk in the chatty and craziness until light and fluffy.
Step 3: Put in a medium-sized baking tin. And turn the oven up but not too high.
Step 4: Place in the oven and bake until golden brown but don't let it sizzle. (If it does sizzle, take out of the oven immediately and leave to cool for an hour).

Step 5: Take out of the oven and leave to cool for 30 minutes.
Step 6: Care for it for 18 years. Enjoy!

Grace Adams (11)
Bervie School, Montrose

This Is Me

Ingredients:
1ml of kindness
399g of pizza
2 guinea pigs
1000g of happiness
2 teaspoons of kickboxing and drama
1 teaspoon of Roblox
Some helpfulness
1 of each colour bell pepper
Food, TV and descendants

How to make me:
Put 1ml of kindness and 399g of pizza in a bowl and then blend
Then add 2 teaspoons of kickboxing and drama and 1 teaspoon of Roblox and mix it a little
Add 1 of each colour bell pepper, chopped up into small pieces, to the bowl and mix
After it has been mixed, add food, TV and descendants and some helpfulness and carefully mix
Then add 1000g of happiness and blend

Put in the oven set to 180°C and bake for five minutes
Then take it out of the oven and add the guinea pigs as decorations.

Rihanna Ross (11)
Bervie School, Montrose

This Is Me

How to make me...

Ingredients:
250g of kindness
3 teaspoons of weirdness
200g of creativity
2 Boost chocolate bars
3ml of video games
1 bowl of happiness
1 loving family
50g of swimming
3 tiny dogs

How to make me:
First, put in the 200g of creativity and the 250g of kindness
Then put in the 2 Boost chocolate bars and 50g of swimming and mix
After it's mixed, add 3ml of video games and then put the 3 teaspoons of weirdness in and mix again
Now put one bowl of happiness in and one loving family

Let it sit for 45 minutes
Then add 3 tiny dogs and mix
Put in the oven for 1 hour
Leave to cool and serve with a hug.

Siena Burton (11)
Bervie School, Montrose

This Is Me

My cat is a super spy,
Jumping from roof to roof,
Chasing the birds that fly,
Now you see him, now he's gone, *poof!*

Angry to happy to sad again,
Sometimes I just need some zen,

Glasses like superhero goggles,
I can see in the dark!
They help me write some fantasy novels,
From far, far away I can see some bark,

My sister, mum and dad,
When they are all around, I am very glad,

As still as a statue, he sits on my bed,
When I'm away, he's guarding my room,
Give it up for Mr Ted!
I like to knit him little hoodies and a costume,

My mood? It just depends,
Depends on my group of crazy friends!

Anna Marie Davies (11)
Bervie School, Montrose

This Is Me

T rain in football every day with my lightning boots scoring goals
H ard-working person is who I am, helping people when I can
I drive the ball in golf like I'm driving a rocket to space
S afe and helpful, helping others whenever I can

I am a super centre mid, bolting towards the sun
S wimming is one of my strongest activities, front crawl is one of my favourite strokes

M anchester United is my favourite team, but closer to home it has to be Aberdeen
E veryone says I'm clumsy and annoying and they are probably right.

Euan Reid (10)
Bervie School, Montrose

Recipe For Me!

To make me, you will need:
Clean bedroom
Shiny brown hair
1kg of happiness
10kg of kindness
A light dusting of ballet
A lot of sweetness
1 tablespoon of smartness

Instructions:
Start by mixing 1kg of happiness and shiny brown hair in the clean bedroom
Then add 10kg of kindness, all of the sweetness and a tablespoon of smartness
After adding, incorporate the rest of the ingredients together
Put the mixture into a 12 x 4 baking tin
Bake for 9 minutes
After baking, add a light dusting of ballet on top and leave to cool
Enjoy!

April Rowe (11)
Bervie School, Montrose

This Is Me

Rugby is my happy place,
Even if I have a frown on my face,
I'm crazy about different brands of cars,
And I play different guitars.

I like Anthony Horowitz's books,
And I have different looks,
I'm as strong as a gorilla,
And when I go on holiday, it's often Manila.

I like computer games,
And candy canes,
I love dirt biking,
I dislike hiking.

I have a special teddy,
His name is Mr Bear and he is very cuddly and always ready,
I love him so much, he doesn't judge,
But he loves eating fudge.

Harvey Parley
Bervie School, Montrose

This Is Me

T his poem is all about me
H ousework is something I hate, tidying my room is as boring as watching paint dry
I am a lover of animals, Lady the dog is my favourite
S trong and quick are my feet when I play tennis

I love colouring, animals are the best pictures
S uper soft and as furry as a pillow, my dog Lady gives the best cuddles

M aths makes me go mad, my thoughts float away
E very night, I like going out with my friends, they make me laugh.

Olivia Beedie
Bervie School, Montrose

All About Me

T his poem is all about me
H obbies are my dislikes
I normally stay inside but when I get outside, I like to swim
S wimming is something I like to do but I can't do it much for now

I don't like going outside, I'm a lot more of an indoor person
S o I stay indoors, I dislike socialising after stuff like school

M y life is a lot, I have had some stuff that seems impossible to survive
E verything you need to know is here, this is me.

Micheal Crighton (11)
Bervie School, Montrose

This Is Me

T he netball team after school is fun but there aren't that many people there
H alloween is exciting but Christmas is more exciting
I like gymnastics because I get to do flips
S piders are very scary

I don't like football and basketball
S ome subjects in school make me sad but art makes me feel better

M y siblings can be very annoying from time to time
E very maths session makes me want to scream.

Amy Gray (11)
Bervie School, Montrose

This Is Me

T he best feeling is to score goals
H ate doing maths and writing
I love to play football
S ome things about me are I'm clumsy and good at football

I don't like watching cricket
S am is my favourite dog because she sits next to you

M y favourite thing about my dog is when you get home, she will have her teddy and give it to you
E very sport I like to do is football, basketball and golf.

Logan Milne
Bervie School, Montrose

This Is Me

T his is me
H elpful, honest and as kind as a gentle cloud
I love my blue eyes as bright as the sky
S uper fast, I sprint down the wing when looking for the goal

I am very sporty but I can be aggressive when I am playing football
S o are my friends, they are crazy, that's why they're so special to me

M y pets are just amazing and so playful
E very evening, I go to see them.

Isla Craig (11)
Bervie School, Montrose

This Is Me

T eddy is my dog, he is the best dog in the world
H e likes to lick you and make you smile
I love football, it's just my life
S coring goals for fun, that's what I do

I 'm like a monster when it comes to kickboxing
S printing to me is heaven, I'm like a rocket shooting through the stars

M aths makes my brain swirl round and round
E very day, I wish it was just PE.

Harrison Taylor (11)
Bervie School, Montrose

This Is Me

T he subject art makes me feel smart
H owever, grammar makes me feel like I've been hammered
I nterested in science describes me
S mall in terms of confidence, I am

I am Albert Einstein reborn
S trangest of all, I am as curious as Isaac Newton

M y best attribute is my orange hair, brighter than the sun
E verything I do is overly calculated because I'm just like that.

Logan Bruce (10)
Bervie School, Montrose

This Is Me

T his is me
H elpful, honest and kind
I love sports, I am as determined as a bear
S urprisingly, football is my absolute favourite, I am a competitive centre mid

I also love animals, especially my proud playful pets
S chool is not my favourite thing though

M y friends are amazing, we enjoy having lots of fun
E very time see them, we are happy.

Poppy Lee Greig (11)
Bervie School, Montrose

This Is Me

I am, unfortunately, as short as a toddler but I am hard to see.
I can be super, super smart but sometimes I just want to break free!
I can play like I'm in an orchestra with my beautiful rhythmic keys.
I have two beautiful fluffy cats but if they want to ask for food, they always plead.
My fine paint brush flowingly glazes my canvas, creating a masterpiece.
I don't like bananas as they give me allergies!

Luca Elders (11)
Bervie School, Montrose

This Is Me

I do it every day, Monday through Friday
Every day, all day
I also like to do it by the bay
I started last year in May
And there is a lot of movement
I always have a little bit of improvement
At the place I go to, I am a student
I help out with the newest
And they are the smoothest
It is the coolest
Sometimes you do it shoeless
When I am doing it, I can be a bit clueless
What is it?

Answer: Dancing.

Linda-Frances Stubbs (10)
Bervie School, Montrose

This Is Me

T he crazy friend, I am
H air long and brown, as smooth as a mirror
I maginative with a fast mind, reader of all kinds
S cared of many things, but silly and short

I am happy and sad, kind as well
S ometimes mad and alone

M any hobbies I have, I want to be a famous author
E yes green and blue, weird and wonderful too!

Lucy McElarney (11)
Bervie School, Montrose

This Is Me

T alking to my friends is important to me
H onesty is something I value
I really enjoy netball and play it on a Wednesday
S ometimes I like my sisters but not always

I fight with them quite a lot, especially Libby
S tacey is mostly my favourite

M y gymnastics club is a lot of fun
E very day I practise my skills.

Abby Hogg (11)
Bervie School, Montrose

This Is Me

I have two legs, long hair and one strong personality
I play football and love cycling too
I enjoy running around with my friends
I like eating pizza and burgers
I talk a lot but like to be on my own sometimes
I love spending time with my friends and family
I have two cats and a dog and I love them very much
Even when they are soaking wet
And when they bring in birds and mice.

Corrie Hillock (11)
Bervie School, Montrose

This Is Me

T alented at putting on fake nails
H alloween is good but Christmas is better
I hate cleaning my room, moving furniture about is the worst part
S hopping in Lush is the best smell

I get annoyed very fast
S piders scare me

M aths hurts my head
E very time my sister comes into my room, I get mad.

Zoey Dziewientkowski-Rae
Bervie School, Montrose

This Is Me

T his is me, as weird as a weevil as kind as a puppy
H appy most of the time, doing art
I am as energetic as a sly fox
S cared of the dark

I am a full-time animal lover
S illy, kind and weird is what I am

M y family is the best
E verything about my friends is amazing, they are great.

Georgia Paton (11)
Bervie School, Montrose

This Is Me

Most of the time, I am tired,
And maths makes my head go on fire.

I like spooky themes,
Kinda like Halloween.

I do golf but am not a great fan,
And I also suck at making plans.

I use my devices most of the time,
But it's hard to do these rhymes.

I like using my imagination,
And giving information.

Leo McNally (11)
Bervie School, Montrose

This Is Me

I am a great sport
I have eleven players
A massive pitch
Big roaring crowds
Two goals at each end
Ninety minutes in a match
A fifteen-minute halftime
You can't touch the ball
Twenty teams in the league
Three points for a win
One for a draw
And zero for a loss
What am I?

Answer: Football.

Ethan Brooks (10)
Bervie School, Montrose

This Is Me

T his is me
H elpful, kind and caring
I like the team Aberdeen
S urprisingly, my dad is a Hibernian supporter

I am a ferocious and fierce defender
S trangely, I wanted to be a superstar striker

M aths makes me really mad!
E ven more than my annoying brother.

Logan Meldrum
Bervie School, Montrose

This Is Me

I am Jack

A nd I live with my mum, dad, brother and sister
M y rabbits make me happy

J obs at school are fun for me
A nd I am awesome at maths and reading
C ooking and going on scary rides I like
K indness is important to me.

Jack Stephens (11)
Bervie School, Montrose

This Is Me

T all is her name
H aha, just kidding
I t's Roxanne although
S ome call her Roxy

I s a dancer at 11
S tarted at 2

M ainly fast but slow is good too
E very week for Tuesday, Wednesday and Thursday too.

Roxanne Taylor (11)
Bervie School, Montrose

This Is Me!

F amily is the best thing
A lthough family can live in different countries, I still love them
M y mum is the best and so is my brother
I love most of my family
L ike my mum, I have blue eyes and
Y ellow hair.

Isla Fergus (11)
Bervie School, Montrose

This Is Me

I have an older brother
I wouldn't wish for another
We like to play games
But we call each other names
We like to play online
But prefer the sunshine
We used to make a den
That's till he turned ten.

Ellis Forshaw (10)
Bervie School, Montrose

Recipe For Joy

One dog
One football
One pizza
One bible
One MTB ride
One Irn Bru
One family

How could I want more?

Jack Garrett (11)
Bervie School, Montrose

Me!

The things that make me happy
Are the things that make me, me,
And the thing that makes me happiest
Is delicious bubble tea,

When it pops in your mouth,
It is as sweet as bubblegum,
It is in my life and without it,
I would cry until I die,

But I also love Pusheen,
Pusheen is as cute as a puppy,
When I snuggle with her,
I feel warm and cosy,
She is a fluffy ball of fur,

The thing that fills me with disgust is ham,
As disgusting as bushy broccoli,
More horrible than pukey peas,

I love and hate these things,
And that makes me unique.

Matilda Goring (9)
Commercial Primary School, Dunfermline

Things That Make Me, Me

Things that make me happy
Are the things that make me, me,
And the thing that makes me happiest
Is Premier League football.

Fun football,
The most fun sport,
Fantastic football,
Boom! into the net, it goes,
Rough football,
As rough as a gorilla,
Funny football,
Hard football,
As hard as a rock,
It's my favourite thing to do!

Things that make me unhappy
Are the things that make me, me,
And the thing that makes me unhappiest
Is dolls.

Dangerous dolls,
Dumb dolls,
Dolls as scary as a nightmare,
Dolls as mean as a demon.

Some people like football,
And some people don't,
Some people play with dolls,
And other people won't.

Sonny Husband (9)
Commercial Primary School, Dunfermline

The Best Food Ever

The things that make me happy
Are the things that make me, me,
And the thing that makes me happiest
Is my favourite drink: bubble tea.

Boba tea is sweet like bubblegum,
And delicious like candyfloss,
The bubbles pop like popping candy,
Brilliant bubbles, sweet and sugary,
It goes *boom!* in my mouth with delicious taste.

Cucumber is as juicy as a pineapple,
It is as wet as a puddle,
Crunchy cucumber,
It goes *pow!* in my mouth,
Refreshing cucumber,
As smooth as a snake,
Cool cucumber,
Keeps me feeling fresh in the sun,

Both things are very delicious,
You might not agree,
But they are delicious to me.

Orla Healy (9)
Commercial Primary School, Dunfermline

This Is Me

The things that make me happy
Are the things that make me, me,
And the thing that makes me happiest
Is my fantastic friends.

They are as awesome as a spider
Making his web,
I feel on top of the world
When my friends are by my side.

One thing that makes me glad
Is juicy cucumber,
As good as crunchy peppers,
As juicy as a big, red, juicy tomato.

There is one food that I hate:
Honey!
It is as sweet
As five full teaspoons of sugar,
It is horrible, terrible and disgusting,
Horrifying honey!

There are good things and bad,
You might feel the same,
I love myself and my life
Because of all these things.

Catalina Ionita (9)
Commercial Primary School, Dunfermline

Amazing Gymnastics

Gigantic gymnastics, the most fun sport,
Fantastic flips like flip-flops,
Amazing and wow!
For me, a piece of cake.

Vaulting, flipping, back flips, front flips,
It's my favourite thing to do,
Even better than eating cake,
Smiling like a happy dog who won a million pounds.

It would be my dream
To be in the Olympics one day,
To be a World Champion,
To represent Great Britain in my own way.

I can picture it now,
Having fun, feeling amazing,
The crowd cheering, clapping, shouting,
Medals clinking against each other.

I feel proud!

Ollie Mitchell (9)
Commercial Primary School, Dunfermline

My Picnic Life

When I see fantastic food,
I run like a cheetah catching its prey,
My prey is my food that comes my way!

One sip of bubble tea,
I feel the popping in my mouth,
It makes me smile like the sun.

Beans are brilliant,
They make my life,
They are like little beetles
With sauce on them.

Eating cake is a piece of cake,
Cake is just incredible,
Yummy like peanut butter.

Bananas are the best,
Curly like a frisbee,
Yellow like the sun.

My life is a picnic,
I love food.

Malin Forrest (9)
Commercial Primary School, Dunfermline

The Roxy Poem

The things that make me happy
Are the things that make me, me,
And the thing that makes me happiest
Is a cute dog named Roxy.

Roxy is a crazy dog,
Full of energy,
She won't stop running
Until she hits the moon.

When we go for a walk,
She won't stop, like a busy ant,
She gets scared of other dogs,
Even small ones with cute toes.

I love my dog,
So fluffy and cute,
I love to cuddle and pet her,
Roxy is the greatest dog in the world,
I will love her forever.

Emily Pentleton (8)
Commercial Primary School, Dunfermline

Fantastic Football

The things that make me happy
Are the things that make me, me,
And the thing that makes me happiest
Is playing football.

Fantastic football makes me work hard,
And run fast toward the goal,
Boom! I scored!

My mum and dad cheer me on,
And they say, "Break a leg!"
They tell me I am amazing,
That I am the best.

Since football is so fantastic,
I want to become a professional,
I would be over the moon!

Dylan Kinninmonth (9)
Commercial Primary School, Dunfermline

The Great Lily

The things that make me happy
Are the things that make me, me,
The thing that makes me happy
Is a cute hamster called Lily.

Lily is a hamster from Russia,
Oh, she is so cute!
She is just like a little kitten,
Oh, she is so cute!
She has a tail like a little stick,
Oh, she is so cute!
Her body is smaller than my hand,
Oh, she is so cute!
She runs on her wheel like a dog,
Oh, she is so cute!

Aaron Leitch (9)
Commercial Primary School, Dunfermline

All About Me

The thing that makes me happiest
Is my fantastic dog called Casey,
As gold as a sparkling gold box,
As sweet as a candy shop.

One thing that makes me happy
Is all of my amazing Prime,
As colourful as a sparkling rainbow,
As sweet as a bag of sugar.

One thing that makes me happy
Is my awesome, sick Xbox,
As black as a bear,
As fun as playing forever.

Now you know all about me.

Dylan Devaney (9)
Commercial Primary School, Dunfermline

My Big Brother

The person who makes me happiest
Is my big brother, Luke,
He's the best brother ever!

Luke is funny, kind and caring,
He has so many friends,
We play Just Dance and Mario
On the Nintendo,
It makes both of us happy.

But Luke is annoying sometimes,
When he says, "It's your turn to do the dishes!"
I hate it, but oh well,
It's what big brothers do.

Lyra Fowles (9)
Commercial Primary School, Dunfermline

Things I Like

The thing that makes me happiest
Is a cute little dog named Clover,
She is the best furry friend in the world,
She is cute, fluffy and very cuddly,
Sometimes, she zooms all over the place,
She's as fluffy as a feather.

I also love my four-year-old sister,
She is friendly and playful,
She is as cute as a button,
She always gets her way,
She would play with Elsa all day.

Imogen Fleetham (9)
Commercial Primary School, Dunfermline

Sports And Me

This is a thing that makes me happy,
It's something I play outside every day,
It makes me really tired,
It is my favourite thing to do,
It is basketball.

Here is one where you practice skills,
And you learn new things,
You get cool gear - a suit and belt,
The belt changes colour as you get better,
I find it as hard as playing chess,
It is karate!

Rory Mellon (9)
Commercial Primary School, Dunfermline

Basketball

The things that make me happy
Are the things that make me, me,
And the thing that makes me, me
Is my favourite sport: basketball.

Everything about it is good,
Swoosh! The sound of scoring in the net,
The hoorays when someone scores
Are like at the end of a marathon.

It's my dream to be a basketball star,
It will make me happy.

Lucas McLaughlin (9)
Commercial Primary School, Dunfermline

My Lovely Cat, Benson

The thing that makes me the happiest
In the whole wide world
Is my cat called Benson.

My cat is as fluffy as a blanket,
As cute as a baby seal,
As energetic as a dog,
As sleepy as a tired sloth,
He makes me feel so loved.

One day, he bit me on my arm,
As fierce as a killer whale,
As ferocious as a tiger,
My best friend, Benson.

Ben Dumble (9)
Commercial Primary School, Dunfermline

Good Life, Bad Life

Pepperoni pizza is delicious,
As delicious as a Wispa, trust me,
I like the stretchy cheese,
And the crispy crust.

But I hate broccoli,
It fills me with disgust,
It is as disgusting as a Brussels sprout,
It is revolting.

Dogs, I love dogs,
Dogs that sleep like logs,
Dogs that look like hogs,
Dogs are as cute as bunny rabbits.

Lyla Leader (9)
Commercial Primary School, Dunfermline

Coco

The things that make me happiest
Are the things that make me, me,
And that is football,
Fantastic football.

Fantastic football,
Fun football,
As fun as a rollercoaster.

My curious dog called Coco,
My own furry ball of happiness,
They are entertaining, fun and playful,
They are the best pet!

Hector Warner (9)
Commercial Primary School, Dunfermline

My Best Friend, Paul

It's nice to have a friend,
And my best buddy is Paul,
He runs as fast as a race car,
Which makes him great at games,
Paul is super loyal,
I'm glad he is my friend.

Toby Serkes (9)
Commercial Primary School, Dunfermline

Maggie The Magicarp

You are as shiny as glistening gold,
You are a spectacular star,
You are as red as the scorching sun,
You are as blue as the vast sea,
You are the best Magicarp in the world!

Tehillah Isaiah (9)
Commercial Primary School, Dunfermline

This Is Me

Shiny dark-chocolate hair, flowing like melted chocolate.
Sea-blue eyes glistening like the sea on a sunny day.
I love the creatures of the forest, they bring a smile in the darkest times like a ball of hope.
My favourite hobby is singing.
My mother says I have the voice of an angel, but I don't think so.
My favourite colour is yellow like lemons.
I love the idea of a small town at the seaside.
My favourite time of the year is the cold, windy and rainy winter because of the warm clothes and sugary sweets, the hot fire on the candles glowing brighter than the rest, the calm scent of wax wafts in the air.
That is what I like.
That is me!

Heather (10)
Crail Primary School, Anstruther

This Is Me

Eyes as brown as a rusted treasure chest,
Hair as brown as a crispy autumn leaf,
Nutella pushes me toward the buffet,
But fish makes me want to stay away.

My village is the size of a shoe,
I love swimming in the ocean when it's sky-blue,
My dog runs around all day,
With as much energy as a jumping bean.

I love sticking my nose in books,
And scavenging for clues,
I love making movies
With all my special friends.

Wallabies and kangaroos
Are my favourite animals in the zoo.
I am as cool as an iceberg
Drifting across the sea.

Crunchy amber carrots
Will bring me joy,

But my little sister
Will just annoy!

This is me!

Ella Molly Drew (11)
Crail Primary School, Anstruther

This Is Me

I really love my cat, he is as fluffy as a pillow.
I am fast but not the fastest when it comes to a race.
My big blue eyes are as blue as the sky.
I really like riding my scooter, it is good exercise.
Pizza is my favourite food, especially pepperoni pizza.
I like playing games on my Xbox a lot, maybe a bit too much!
I like playing on my trampoline, I jump a lot on it.
I really like maths, I always try my hardest on it.
My hair is as brown as Nutella chocolate.
I really like going on holiday, it's a lot of fun.
I like my parents more than anyone else.
This is me.

Brodie Wilson (10)
Crail Primary School, Anstruther

This Is Me

My dark hair is like melted Nutella,
My hazelnut eyes are big and bold.
My favourite food is steaming-hot steak,
With juicy chips.
My favourite drink is hot chocolate,
With sweet-tasting marshmallows.
My favourite sport is football,
I'm a pack of lions attacking on the wing.
My favourite footballer is Ronaldo,
He smacks the ball into the top corner.
My favourite animal is a cheetah,
Because they are fast like me!
My favourite colour is bright red,
It is a ball of fire.
I love the woods,
They are mysterious and dark,
I love the feeling of being scared when exploring them.

Edward Robertson (10)
Crail Primary School, Anstruther

This Is Me

My eyes are green emeralds
Shining in the night sky.
Dark hazelnut hair.
I am as cool as an iceberg.

I love to swim in the fresh sea.
My skin is white chocolate.
I love to play with my friends.
I am a karate master.
I like playing the drums as loud as I can.

My dog, Dave, brown as a tree trunk.
I like walking him rain or shine.
My dog can run as fast as a Tesla.

I love eating carrots because they make me see in the dark.
Love watching movies with my family.
I am good at drawing.

Euan Cochrane (10)
Crail Primary School, Anstruther

This Is Me

My eyes are as green as the summer trees,
My hair is brown like gooey melted chocolate,
My skin is tanned like I have been left in the sun for days,

I am a superstar at horse riding,
When I canter around the whole arena, I feel very proud,

My cat is snowy and bright,
My favourite food is warm and soft rice balls,
I always ride my bike in my free time,

I love to draw,
It is like creating a whole world,
My favourite season is autumn,
I like the dry leaves crunching under my boots.

Julianna J (10)
Crail Primary School, Anstruther

This Is Me

My eyes are as blue as the sea in Florida,
Looking left and right no matter what,
I am wary like an owl in the dark, hunting for its prey,
I have the eye of a tiger.

I love pandas!
The big, furry, dark black and pure white fur,
So big to cuddle and pet,
My favourite animal, they feast upon stacks of bamboo.

I'm as happy as can be,
Having a happy life, living with my wonderful family,
I feel like I could just dance,
Getting spoiled by my good, young, yes not old, granny!

Andy Grant (10)
Crail Primary School, Anstruther

This Is Me

I have dark brown, oak hair,
My eyes are like the ocean,
My skin is maple syrup,

My favourite thing is football,
I feel energised when I pass the ball,

My favourite food is pepperoni pizza,
It is cheesy and stringy,

My favourite season is summer,
It is burning hot,

My favourite animal is a cheetah,
They are fast like me,

My favourite mythical animal is a dragon,
It breathes red lava fire.

Taylor B (10)
Crail Primary School, Anstruther

This Is Me

What you will need to make me:
A pinch of golden shimmer,
Teaspoon full of seawater,
1 million doughnuts with sticky, gooey, slimy jam,
My amazing fluffy dog Toby, toffee-brown with dark-chocolate coating,
My besties make me feel amazing when they are near,
My dad's hotdogs, crunchy in the middle, soft on the outside.

Method:
Mix all these ingredients together and what do you get?
Me!

Matylda Kubecka (11)
Crail Primary School, Anstruther

This Is Me

My hair is blueberries,
My eyes look like green grapes,
My skin is glowing,
I am as fast as a lightning bolt running up and down the pitch,
Striking goals in the back of the net.

My pet is a fluffy ball like a tiny, cute mouse,
But on the inside, it is an evil beast,
Waiting to nibble fingers,
I love Roblox Blox Fruits,
I feel like a strong pirate with a sabre sword when I play.

Zach Taylor (11)
Crail Primary School, Anstruther

This Is Me

My hair is caramel and milk chocolate.
My eyes are as green as Nigeria's flag.
My skin is as shiny as gold.
When I play football, I feel like a lightning bolt on the wing.
I am so good at football, I am like a god.
When I do a skill goal, it makes me feel victorious.
My favourite food is pizza, it tastes like cheese heaven.

Kristians J (9)
Crail Primary School, Anstruther

This Is Me

This is me.
My eyes are as blue as the sky.
My hair is light as white chocolate.
My dog has pale smooth skin.
My favourite thing is parkour at the sandy rocky beach.
My favourite sport is football, I am a super player.
I like video games, Xbox is my favourite.
I am good at playing with my best friends in the cool autumn.

Lewis Ireland (9)
Crail Primary School, Anstruther

This Is Me

I love dogs!
My first ever pet,
Ears as big as an elephant's,
Nose wetter than a frog,
Loves anybody, no matter where they're from.

I love dinosaurs!
Long, feathered bodies,
Flat snouts and sharp teeth,
Sickle-shaped claws for slicing,
Deinonychus means 'terrible claw'.

Rupert (10)
Crail Primary School, Anstruther

This Is Me

My hair is like the night sky.
My eyes are like chocolate doughnuts.
My skin is tanned, it went white to blackish.
My favourite food is pink, sprinkled doughnuts.
My favourite colours are deep, ocean, dark blue and black, like ink.
My favourite things to do are play Xbox and go outside and sleep.

Oscar F (9)
Crail Primary School, Anstruther

This Is Me

My teeth are white.
My skin is sand.
My hair is as dark as oak.
My eyes are as blue as the sea.
My lips are red and pink.
My heart is red.
My tongue is reddish pink.
I love cats because they are cute.
I love dogs because they are small.

Lucas Yule (10)
Crail Primary School, Anstruther

This Is Me

Add a pinch of dark caramel.
Add a couple of waves.
My freckles are cookies melting into my skin.
My favourite thing is winning with my team in football.
I fall into a different world of pain.
I play video games on my TV that buzz!

Max M (10)
Crail Primary School, Anstruther

A Recipe For Whitechin

Gather toys with catnip and food, fidget toys and IQ toys.
Add a sprinkle of energy.
Pour in catnip and love and sweetness and goodness with a sweet smell.
Add a warm blanket with love and care and a bit of catnip.
Blend snuggles that are warm like gentle mittens.
Blend all of it together with love and do it again to give him warmth.
If he has a good snuggle, he gets treats in return.
If I'm sad, he makes me happy and he will make you too.
Warm with his favourite milk for when he feels blue.

Elli-Mae (9)
Gorsewood Primary School, Runcorn

A Recipe For Millie

First, gather loveliness and cuteness,
Stir in a massive bag of love and Starbucks,
Season with Mum and Dad and Nan Townsend,
Add a pinch of home, sweets and pizza,
Pour in a lot of kindness and money,
Add my rabbit, Christmas, Taylor Swift, Ste Cook and shoes,
Blend in Stitch and Angel, bed and my favourite apps,
Then warm gently with puppy dog eyes and looking cute.

Millie Townsend (9)
Gorsewood Primary School, Runcorn

A Recipe For Shankley

First, gather love and kisses,
Stir in all sorts of favourite toys,
Season with friends and family,
Add a pinch of curiosity,
Pour in a galaxy full of strokes and cuteness,
And food, bed and walks,
Blend braveness and playfulness and smartness,
Then warm gently by saying, "Bath time and tea time!" and "When I say it I mean it!"

Elle Woods (9)
Gorsewood Primary School, Runcorn

A Recipe For Rosalie

First, gather kindness and the loveliest smile,
Stir in a lot of fun,
Season with hugs and kisses,
Add a pinch of running around on a sunny day,
Pour in a cup of the best teddies,
And a touch of adorableness,
Blend friends and family together for love,
Then warm gently by saying, "You are the best little sister in the world!"

Eliza Bennett (9)
Gorsewood Primary School, Runcorn

A Recipe For Me

First, gather sweets and football boots,
Stir in cuddly movie night with popcorn,
Season with fun and energy,
Add a pinch of football and games,
Pour in an ocean load of kindness,
And a pinch of love,
Blend a love for football and accuracy and a bit of literacy,
Then warm gently by adding a bit of a sleeping fish.

Lenny Banks (9)
Gorsewood Primary School, Runcorn

A Recipe For Erikka

First, gather Pringles and chocolate,
Stir in edible money and sweets,
Season with fun and energy,
Add a pinch of cheese and love,
Pour in Halloween, art, running, Aphmau,
And Roblox,
Blend play dough, books, hide-and-seek, rock climbing and adventures,
Then warm gently by adding music, reading, tag and running.

Erikka Pearson-Savage (9)
Gorsewood Primary School, Runcorn

A Recipe For Tegan

First, gather fun and silliness,
Stir in Take That and Olly Murs,
Season with TikTok and Starbucks,
A pinch of One Direction and dancing,
Pour in Robbie Williams and Gary Barlow,
And Ed Sheeran and Lewis Capaldi,
Blend hot sauce and hot noodles - I will eat it in one go,
Then warm with a gentle hug goodbye.

Tegan Probert Groom (10)
Gorsewood Primary School, Runcorn

A Recipe For Alex

First, gather Fireman Sam and jumping,
Stir in cuddles and kissing,
Season with swimming, exploring and cuteness,
Add a pinch of funny and silliness,
Pour in more Fireman Sam toys,
And don't forget a big hug when you need it,
Blend love and affection,
Warm gently by saying, "Party!"

Hayley Neill (10)
Gorsewood Primary School, Runcorn

A Recipe For Jax

First, gather running and fetching,
Stir in fast and kissable,
Season with licking me and cuddles,
Add a pinch of ripping things up,
Pour in walks and games,
And being soft and huggable,
Blend sloppy licks and being squashed and eating bacon,
Then warm gently using puppy eyes for sneaky treats.

Kylan Pearson-Savage
Gorsewood Primary School, Runcorn

A Recipe For Me

First, gather bravery and questions,
Stir in curiosity and fun,
Season with eating, sleeping and games,
Add a pinch of dreams and hopes,
Pour in kindness and coolness,
And swimming and football,
Blend parties and eating and adventures and games,
Then warm gently with basketball and dodgeball.

Charlie Sharp (9)
Gorsewood Primary School, Runcorn

A Recipe For Jayden

First, gather kindness and bravery.
Stir in gaming and swimming.
Season with board games and drawing.
Add a pinch of dancing and drama.
Pour in an earth-load of funniness.
And some climbing to the side.
Blend a guitar and a saxophone.
Then warm gently by having adventures all over the world.

Jayden Yesilyurt (9)
Gorsewood Primary School, Runcorn

A Recipe For My Hamsters

First, gather hamster treats and love,
Stir in a tub of chew toys,
Season with energy and happiness,
Add a pinch of cuteness,
Pour in a tub of silliness,
And my hamsters' warm, cosy cage,
Blend kindness and hugs and cuteness and love,
Then warm gently by giving my hamsters a big hug.

Charlie Mitchell (9)
Gorsewood Primary School, Runcorn

A Recipe For My Puppy Fleur

First, gather treats and cuteness,
Stir in favourite toys and kisses,
Season with walks and cuddles,
Add a pinch of curiosity,
Pour in a bucket of love and warm fur that is soft like a soft blanket,
Blend in treats and food and training and love,
Gently warm with long walks in the park.

Laila Findlow (9)
Gorsewood Primary School, Runcorn

A Recipe For Scarlett

First, gather love and kindness,
Season with energy and love,
Add a pinch of wonderfulness,
Pour in an ocean of resilience,
And add some respect,
Blend in kindness and peacefulness and playfulness and joyfulness,
Then warm gently by playing football, netball and gymnastics.

Scarlett Disberry (9)
Gorsewood Primary School, Runcorn

A Recipe For Mum

First, gather hugs and kindness.
Stir in film nights, hugs and kisses.
Season with toys and games.
Add a pinch of love and fun.
Pour in an ocean full of love and a sea full of wonder.
Blend in family and love.
Then warm gently with the stars from a galaxy full of trust.

James Jones (9)
Gorsewood Primary School, Runcorn

A Recipe For Me

First, gather loudness and goofiness,
Stir in movie nights,
Season with exploring, friends and family,
Add a pinch of music,
Pour in quadrobics,
And energy bursts,
Blend a love for margays, foxes and calmness,
Then warm gently by adding a touch of random laughter.

Karli Rotherham (9)
Gorsewood Primary School, Runcorn

A Recipe For A Dog Called Wally

First, gather dog food and kindness,
Stir in kindness and dog food,
Season with ball games and energy,
Add a pinch of a good boy and cuties,
Pour in a tub of silliness,
And my dog bed,
Blend kindness and cuteness and love,
Then warm gently by cuddling my dog.

Logan Clarke (9)
Gorsewood Primary School, Runcorn

A Recipe For Dad

First, gather cuddles, kisses,
Stir in with Netflix and kindness,
Season with the gym and cheese on toast,
Add a pinch of love,
Pour in wonderful adventures,
And add love,
Blend in peaceful and beautiful animals,
Then warm gently and cuddle.

Sophie Lawrence (8)
Gorsewood Primary School, Runcorn

I Am Able

I think I am able

A rtistic, an architect, an astronomer
M aybe aesthetically amazing

A nd who knows?
B lindingly lavish
L onging for more
E ven drawing things that can't be drawn.

I am able,
I am humorous,
I am articulate,
I am not all great,
Well, in some sort of way.

I think I am able

A ble to rise
M aybe just different

A nd actually brilliant
B eautiful, I think
L ight in the sun
E ven though I can be rude,

Everything is true!

Rumaysa Suffyan (11)
Harris Primary Academy Chafford Hundred, Grays

This Is Me

This is me,
I'm kind and funny,
But my mind is on more money!
I love horses, cats and playing with my friends,
Though I'm scared of everything - the list, it never ends!

I love being happy, but not when people get too clappy,
Although I hate being dirty, I don't mind the mud!
And I'm always in the mood for a meaningful hug.

Some people think I'm bright, some don't but that's alright,
I love Christmas, birthdays, if you didn't know!
I've tried to start a business and it wasn't a game to play!

Lucia Bushell (11)
Harris Primary Academy Chafford Hundred, Grays

This Is My Life

T ime flies quick for me
H aving a ton of homework every week
I love sports, especially football
S eparate progress is for me

I hate doing homework
S ometimes I like to do boring stuff

M aybe sports are not exactly for me
Y oung people think that olives don't taste good, I like them

L ots of boredom during school
I love riding my bike and riding in cars
F ollowing my path in football is my target
E very day, I go to school late.

Petar Borisov (10)
Harris Primary Academy Chafford Hundred, Grays

Making Me

I love my hamster,
I love my friends,
I love my mum,
And I love sports!

I dislike swimming,
I dislike sushi,
I dislike history,
And I dislike rock music!

I am kind,
I am generous,
I am sporty,
I am hardworking!

I love the beach,
I love the stars,
I love the sky,
And I love the sun!

I love to shop,
I love to draw,

I love to dance,
And I love to sing!

We need diversity!
We need love!
We need kindness!
And we need me!

Kyla Ocean (10)
Harris Primary Academy Chafford Hundred, Grays

Carla

Wait, who is Carla?
I'm Carla!
I love cats,
And I could eat a Big Mac!

There are ten billion bunnies,
But which one is funny?
Who's the bunny, I'm the bunny!

I like to be funny, I like to act,
So what role shall I choose?
I've got no clue...
My brain is like an air balloon!

Whenever you're down, I'll bring you back up,
Chase your dreams, you know I'm not mean!
Carla is nice, Carla can be mean,
But that's in the times when nobody can ever breathe!

Carla Popa (9)
Harris Primary Academy Chafford Hundred, Grays

Just A Young Boy With Dreams

Just a young boy with dreams,
Trying to make it pro without saying no.
It's just going to get harder,
But my dreams will keep getting larger.
I'm doing it to make my family proud,
So I can say I made it out loud.
I want to be a footballer,
I know I will make it, I have to believe,
My dream is not a want, it's a need.
Every time I fall down, I will get back up,
Because this is my dream and I never give up.
I want to go from playing in the streets,
To playing in front of 40,000 seats.

Kyron Mudhar (11)
Harris Primary Academy Chafford Hundred, Grays

This Is My Life

My refuge feels like jumping onto a soft, comfy bed
On Christmas eve,
Dug under the warm, thick blanket.

My refuge smells like a warm scented candle
Colliding with the windless air
At home.

My refuge sounds like waking up on a new dawn
In spring,
The sound of birds chirping around me.

My refuge looks like the wild flowers
In my garden,
Sleeping around the palm tree.

My refuge tastes like the fresh-baked gingerbread cookies
With cinnamon breaching the top.

Dovydas Dula (11)
Harris Primary Academy Chafford Hundred, Grays

Me, A Gem

When I close my eyes,
Moonlight shimmers everywhere,
Phoenixes and falcons circle the sky,
A sapphire in my dark hair.

When I read, I read a book,
The characters come out and beckon to me,
Maybe high in an aeroplane,
Or at the bottom of an azure sea.

When I'm fast asleep,
Cold and all alone,
I dream of lands where hope soars high,
My one and only home.

Just remember this,
People beg and plead
Just to get a life
Where they can be free.

Joannabel Emma Eshun (10)
Harris Primary Academy Chafford Hundred, Grays

You May Know Myself

Started this game on the 19th of February,
Am I lame? I say quite the contrary,
School is where I go ABCDEFG,
Like where my friends are full of glee,
Despise climate change,
Because it makes me want to rage,
Favourite animal is a penguin,
You know how they widdle waddle,
In other words, we shouldn't diddle daddle,
Like how I want to be an engineer,
Succeeding in all my peers,
With that, there are some fears,
But my future has to be clear.

Kouami Zewu-Manscour (10)
Harris Primary Academy Chafford Hundred, Grays

A Recipe Poem All About Me

To create me, you will need:
A tablespoon of creativity,
A slab of confidence,
10lbs of mischief,
A pinch of passion,
A dash of glow to be ready to go.

Now you will need to:
Add 10lbs of mischief,
Mix in a tablespoon of creativity,
Stir in roughly while adding a slab of confidence,
Next, add a pinch of passion and glow,
Spread the mix neatly over a tray of baking paper,
Sprinkle on happiness and leave it to cool down,
This is me!

Karinna Maria Pirvu (10)
Harris Primary Academy Chafford Hundred, Grays

When I Play Netball

When I play netball, I use a ball,
When I play netball, I am never that tall,
When I play netball, I never normally run,
When I play netball, I never chew gum.

When I play some netball, I sometimes play on my own,
When I look up some tips, I look them up on Google Chrome,
When I play netball, I am always positive,
When I'm in a match, I am always competitive.

When I play, I always use a trick,
When I play, I am always ecstatic.

Mason McLintock (10)
Harris Primary Academy Chafford Hundred, Grays

How To Create Me

To create me, you will need:
A sprinkle of confidence,
A pinch of hope,
A dash of happiness,
A tablespoon of kindness,
Half a tablespoon of anger,
A bit of sadness,
Add 10 tablespoons of fun and mischief,
And a whole lot of family and friends.

Now you will need to:
Add half a pinch of shyness,
A spoonful of brightness,
Mix it all,
Put it in the oven,
Wait for 30 minutes,
And there you have me!

Saanvi Bolisetty (10)
Harris Primary Academy Chafford Hundred, Grays

This Is Me

I'm a creative of the land
And I'm handsome,
I'm a creature that cannot fly
But I'm still awesome,
I'm the start of a new evolution,
Which involves class,
I'm the smartest of them all,
And I always pass,
I'm the fastest of them all
And I don't even use all of my class,
They call me Megamind,
But I'm not a villain,
Obey your Head Boy,
As I'm so thrilling!
This is me!

Zac Charova (10)
Harris Primary Academy Chafford Hundred, Grays

This Is Me

This is me
I like tea
This is me
I play for a team
I am quick-minded
And I love rhyming
I don't care about what people say
I just go my way
I might be hated
But I won't be rated
My mum is my fave
And pizza is my crave
I might be lazy
But I will always remain crazy
I have a passion
To have fashion
I'm a big guy
And I am an island
This is me
And the best of me.

Jovani Junaid (9)
Harris Primary Academy Chafford Hundred, Grays

How To Make Idil

10 litres of loving and caring,
A sprinkle of happiness,
Dump in outgoing, fun, kind and generous,
A pinch of love for swimming, dancing and acting,
Dump in caring for family, friends and others.

Now you need to:
Add 10 litres of loving and caring,
A sprinkle of happiness,
Now mix,
Dump in caring for family and friends and others,
A pinch of love for swimming, dancing and acting,
This is me.

Idil Tunc (10)
Harris Primary Academy Chafford Hundred, Grays

The Reality Of My Family

Two houses, two homes, two kitchens, two phones, two couches.
Where I lay, two places that I stay.
Moving and moving, I'm always somewhere
From Monday to Sunday I'm everywhere.
I want to live the nuclear life
With a happy dad and his loving wife.
But that's just a dream.
I can't cry, I cannot even scream
So here I sit with cat number 3,
Life would be easier if there were two of me.

Daisy Santos (10)
Harris Primary Academy Chafford Hundred, Grays

My Refuge Is...

My refuge feels like a silky soft pillow of comfort and safety,
My refuge smells like the fresh air and grass scent on a field,
My refuge sounds like the soft laughter on the beach filling up the air,
My refuge looks like a clear blue sky with seagulls flying around and the sun shining in the sky,
My refuge tastes like the cool ice cream on a hot sunny day at the seaside, with the freedom and safety of a bird.

Nathan Chau (11)
Harris Primary Academy Chafford Hundred, Grays

Me And Riding Rollercoasters

R iding rollercoasters
I have so much fun
D ing!
I t is scary
N ibbles of fun
G old coins

C oasters full of fun
O minous rides
A ride full of memories
S o many coasters
T he rides full of happy endings
E ndings of memories
R inging the bell
S aying hooray!

Tanveer Khan (9)
Harris Primary Academy Chafford Hundred, Grays

This Is Me

T iny in size with giant personality
H ave so many friends
I love eating all my favourite foods
S ounds that are too loud make me annoyed

I play on my PlayStation with my friends
S o much fun I have every day

M e and my friends love playing together
E verything is so fun with all my friends.

Timilehion Rufai (11)
Harris Primary Academy Chafford Hundred, Grays

This Is Who I Am

A girl with dreams,
Who is kind as can be,
This is who I am
Forever to be,

A girl who is caring,
Also very loving,
This is who I am,
It is special to me,

I'm powerful and unstoppable,
I know it is possible,

I can be a singer,
Or help people's rights,
This is who I am,
And I like it this way.

Casey Otieno (10)
Harris Primary Academy Chafford Hundred, Grays

This Is Me

This is me,
I'm Idris Akanbi,
I am always full of glee,
I love to eat spaghetti,

I play basketball,
And I'm a little tall,
I love going to the mall,
My favourite season is fall,

I love my family,
I like the flower lily,
I love the colour green,
My school is Harris Academy,
This is me.

Idris Akanbi (10)
Harris Primary Academy Chafford Hundred, Grays

This Is Me

T he young child who loves gaming
H as missed a once-in-a-lifetime opportunity
I love going on road trips
S ometimes practises football with his dad

I never come to school late
S ometimes make friends

M e and my friends get many wins
E veryone knows I like mints.

George Raducanu (10)
Harris Primary Academy Chafford Hundred, Grays

This Is Me

T wo years later, I met my new friends
H ave a really kind parent
I love my brother and dog that care about me
S easide is my favourite place

I really like playing games
S ometimes I play with my friends

M e and my friend have lots of fun
E njoying ourselves.

Daniel Sosnowski (11)
Harris Primary Academy Chafford Hundred, Grays

This Is Me

All I can ever see is what is in front of me.
I like to drink tea and eat Oreos on the settee.
I go up to my bedroom and lay on my bed 'cause I usually have a sore head.
I like horror so I draw a flesh-eating boar.
I don't like to travel because it is a bit hard for me to handle.

This is me.
The best I can be!

James Michel Thomas (9)
Harris Primary Academy Chafford Hundred, Grays

This Is Me

I am a competitive swimmer,
Brave, loving and a singer,
Supporting the school, I am a footballer,
Caring for my animals, I am a helper.

I love to eat, which makes me an eater,
I am always wishing, which makes me a dreamer,
I adore the night, which makes me a sleeper,
I admire the TV, which makes me a watcher.

Emily Georgieva (10)
Harris Primary Academy Chafford Hundred, Grays

This Is How I Am Myself

T omorrow is going to be better than today.
H ooray, it is the weekend.
I love to be myself.
S unshine helps me rhyme.

I love my family.
S ometimes I make mistakes but it helps me learn.

M y life is filled with happiness.
E nd of my poem... This is me!

Taqwa Khan (8)
Harris Primary Academy Chafford Hundred, Grays

How To Make Me

Short height,
Black curly hair,
Athletics,
Swimming and music,
Lana del Ray,
Bubble tea,
Cats,
Overthinker,
Fearful,
Positive,
Anger issues.

Method:
First, get a clean bowl,
Add a cup of short height and some black curly hair,
Well done, you have now made my appearance!

Brielle Okparaocha (10)
Harris Primary Academy Chafford Hundred, Grays

I Am

I am aesthetic as a rainbow,
I am a dancer - not a singer!
I am sweet but shy,
I am more nervous than the nervous system,
I am never in trouble because I'm silent!
My forehead is so big just because I'm smart!
I am a gamer but still like football,
I like my writing but not my drawing,
This is me.

Igor Karagiaz (11)
Harris Primary Academy Chafford Hundred, Grays

Me

I'm inspired by Ariana Grande, Zendaya and gymnasts,
I'm from Italy and Albania,
And I might start my own business,
My parents are my saviours,
And I enjoy presents on Christmas.

I like pizza, cucumber, burgers and cake,
I dislike soup,
Cookies, I can make,
Although, I'm a noob!

Oreida Pashaj (10)
Harris Primary Academy Chafford Hundred, Grays

A Recipe Poem

To create me, we will need:
A book filled with happiness,
A slab of cheesy pizza,
85lbs of fun,
A pinch of mischief,
A slice of pizza,
A bedroom filled with games.

Now you need to:
Add 25lbs of mischief,
Add a sprinkle of kind,
Add a lot of anger,
This is me!

Lewis Fern (10)
Harris Primary Academy Chafford Hundred, Grays

My Refuge

My refuge feels like the velvety smooth blanket to cover me in safety,
My refuge smells like the fresh air of comfort,
My refuge sounds like the laughter of me and my friends and family,
My refuge looks like the clear, blue, crystal sky telling me I have hope and freedom,
My refuge tastes like trust.

Adel Awoyemi (11)
Harris Primary Academy Chafford Hundred, Grays

The Summer Recipe

How to make me:
First, add a bit of gymnastics,
Then put in a bit of sushi,
Next, add a pinch of books,
After some books, add drawing,
And now add 10lbs of fun and fashion,
Add some happiness,
Then some teddies,
After, mix until you see bubbles,
And now you have made me!

Summer Dam (10)
Harris Primary Academy Chafford Hundred, Grays

My Teddy

My refuge is a teddy,
Sweet, comforting and protective,
A heartwarming and lovely teddy.

Always is a sweet teddy,
Glorious, wistful and sweet,
The softest thing in refuge.

A welcoming boy called Lost,
Loving, caring and sporty,
The best in the world.

Timas Miknevicius (10)
Harris Primary Academy Chafford Hundred, Grays

My Refuge

My refuge is a moon,
Bright, gorgeous and welcoming,
An understanding angel-like person.

My refuge is a sunset,
Ombre, hopeful and pretty,
As it stands up for itself.

My refuge is a cloud,
Soft, delicate and welcoming,
A fallen angel that stands out.

Leila Martynenko (11)
Harris Primary Academy Chafford Hundred, Grays

This Is Me

This is me,
My name is Sophie,
I like to sing,
I am a kind person,
And like to find positivity,
I'm determined in cheer,
And hope to overcome a fear,
I am caring and daring,
Yet sometimes a little dull,
I have to find the light
To seem bright.

Sophie Chapman (11)
Harris Primary Academy Chafford Hundred, Grays

My Safe Zone

My refuge is a bear,
Soft, silky and warm,
Someone I will trust forever.

My refuge is the ocean,
Calm, glowy and bright,
An understanding breeze of reason.

My refuge is the weather,
Unexpected, sweet and harsh,
Something with a peaceful mind.

Helena Rose (10)
Harris Primary Academy Chafford Hundred, Grays

My Happy Place

My refuge is a wave,
Bright, beautiful and bold,
Calmness on a rough day.

My refuge is a sunset,
Warm, cosy and comfortable,
Helpful on a stormy day.

My refuge is my happiness,
Heartwarming, healing and healthy,
Honest in a bad situation.

Michaela Somuyiva (11)
Harris Primary Academy Chafford Hundred, Grays

This Is Me

To create me, you will need:
A book reader,
A painter or an artist,
A good swimmer,
And a drawer,
A happy person,
Or a down person,
But you don't need the sixth one
Because I'm never down,
A smart kid,
A quiet kid,
This is me!

Poppy Maydell (10)
Harris Primary Academy Chafford Hundred, Grays

My Refuge

My refuge is concrete walls,
Protective, safe and strong,
Allowing me to focus always.

My refuge is a bubble,
Sturdy, warm and bright,
A way to ease myself.

My refuge is my friend,
Kind, honest and loving,
A light in my day.

MJ Nee-Whang (10)
Harris Primary Academy Chafford Hundred, Grays

All About Me

I am a good runner,
As well as a fast swimmer,
I love good food,
And eat a lot too,
I like to game,
And have good aim,
I am young and small,
But smart and strong,
I like to sleep,
Also to wake up early,
This is all about me.

Dawud Shahzad (10)
Harris Primary Academy Chafford Hundred, Grays

This Is Me

T angerines are my favourite fruit
H ave two cats in my house
I am a Muslim
S o fun in school

I have a brother
S ister, I have

M y brother is taller than my mum
E nd of poem.

Mahad Hassan (10)
Harris Primary Academy Chafford Hundred, Grays

Who Or What Am I?

I am smart,
I am bold,
I am kind,
I am confident,
I create and make,
I dream big and reach for the stars,
I am a bookworm - a reader of many things,
I am part chocolate and pizza,
What am I?
I am me and me is who I want to be.

Favor Mwafulirwa (10)
Harris Primary Academy Chafford Hundred, Grays

This Is Me

My favourite singer is Taylor Swift,
I always thought I was born with a gift,
A gift of drawing,
Every day in my life, I'm scoring,
Although most of it is boring,
I like cooking,
I like drawing,
But I'm not a big fan of running.

Ava Puri (10)
Harris Primary Academy Chafford Hundred, Grays

My Refuge Is...

My refuge is an angel,
Lovable, caring and careful,
I loved it very much.

My refuge is a god,
Loving, kind and caring,
It is my favourite thing.

My refuge is the best,
Bright, welcoming, helpful,
I love it very much.

Harmony (10)
Harris Primary Academy Chafford Hundred, Grays

Kennings Poem

I am a...
Heavy sleeper,
Wasp fleer,
Tennis beater,
Football beater,
Big eater,
Light beater,
Night sleeper,
Low throw,
Ho ho!
Look to my left,
Look to my right,
And say goodnight.

Ronnie Horning (11)
Harris Primary Academy Chafford Hundred, Grays

This Is Me

I am a strong player,
I am a fast defender,
I am a sprinter,
I am a nice player,
I am a star,
I am a sleeper,
I am a fast sleeper,
I am a chocolate eater,
I am a super striker,
This is me!

Ridwan Bada (10)
Harris Primary Academy Chafford Hundred, Grays

I Am A...

A kennings poem

I am a...
Football watcher,
Deep sleeper,
Book reader,
Goalkeeper,
Fast walker,
Fast attacker,
Small shopper,
Fantastic gamer,
And finally,
I am a good helper,
This is me.

Frank Wojnarowski (10)
Harris Primary Academy Chafford Hundred, Grays

This Is Me

My interest is video games,
I like playing football games,
I love food but my friend thinks it is lame,
I am a sporty kid,
I love penguins, I find them cool,
I also love going and playing in the pool.

Arash Khan (10)
Harris Primary Academy Chafford Hundred, Grays

All About Me

My refuge feels like a warm, hot day
On the beach, playing in the sand.

My refuge smells like the amazing food
My mum cooks.

My refuge sounds like a mythical rushing
Upon the sea shore.

Abdul-Wadood Bello (10)
Harris Primary Academy Chafford Hundred, Grays

This Is Me

A kennings poem

I am a...
Footballer,
Game player,
Wasp killer,
Sandwich maker,
Book reader,
Big sleeper,
Early riser,
Chocolate eater,
Fast eater,
Active player,
Overthinker.

Hannas Aina (11)
Harris Primary Academy Chafford Hundred, Grays

My Life So Far

Every day in my life
Feels like a normal day,
Thinking about…

Thinking of memories,
I can forget
In a few years.

Every step I take
Makes me think
Of my life.

Abhinav Chris Chakka (10)
Harris Primary Academy Chafford Hundred, Grays

This Is Me

I am a...
Funny,
Kind,
Caring,
Sometimes positive,
Confident,
Clumsy,
Good helper,
Happy,
Smart,
Get scared very easily,
Silly,
This is me.

Surayya Houssein (10)
Harris Primary Academy Chafford Hundred, Grays

This Is Me

A kennings poem

I am a…
Big sleeper,
Football watcher,
Book reader,
Chocolate eater,
Winter wisher,
Bread and jam maker,
Early riser,
Game player,
This is me.

Stefan Olaru (10)
Harris Primary Academy Chafford Hundred, Grays

All About Me

I am the courageous thinker with a hint of creativity,
I am the thoughtful wisher,
I am the book reader,
I am a creative drawer,
I love sushi, ramen and boba.

Yasmin Al-Saadi (11)
Harris Primary Academy Chafford Hundred, Grays

This Is Me

Humans are destroying the environment,
We could ask for help from the government,
We need to go save the wildlife,
We need to go do it right now for life.

Vakaris Niparavicius (11)
Harris Primary Academy Chafford Hundred, Grays

This Is Me

I am a...
Hard sleeper,
Sporty,
Fast,
Active person,
Likes maths,
Football lover,
Likes games,
Mostly out.

Kristupas Andriuska (10)
Harris Primary Academy Chafford Hundred, Grays

YOUNG WRITERS INFORMATION

We hope you have enjoyed reading this book – and that you will continue to in the coming years.

If you're the parent or family member of an enthusiastic poet or story writer, do visit our website **www.youngwriters.co.uk/subscribe** and sign up to receive news, competitions, writing challenges and tips, activities and much, much more! There's lots to keep budding writers motivated!

If you would like to order further copies of this book, or any of our other titles, then please give us a call or order via your online account.

Young Writers
Remus House
Coltsfoot Drive
Peterborough
PE2 9BF
(01733) 890066
info@youngwriters.co.uk

Join in the conversation!
Tips, news, giveaways and much more!

YoungWritersUK   YoungWritersCW   youngwriterscw

Scan me to watch the This Is Me video!